Provided
by

Measure B

which was approved by
the voters in
November, 1998

"Every slave is a stolen man; every slaveholder is a man stealer."

—WILLIAM LLOYD GARRISON

ABOLITIONISTS:
A FORCE FOR CHANGE

By Sarah E. De Capua

Published in the United States of America by The Child's World®
PO Box 326
Chanhassen, MN 55317-0326
800-599-READ
www.childsworld.com

The Child's World®: Mary Berendes, Publishing Director
Editorial Directions, Inc.: E. Russell Primm, Emily Dolbear, Lucia Raatma
and Sarah E. De Capua, Editors; Linda S. Koutris, Photo Selector; Alice Flanagan,
Photo Research; Red Line Editorial, Fact Research; Tim Griffin/IndexServ, Indexer;
Melissa McDaniel, Proofreader

Cover photograph: Portraits of eminent opponents of slavery/ © Bettmann/Corbis

Interior photographs ©: Corbis: 11, 16; Bettmann/Corbis: 2, 18, 25, 26, 28 right, 33; Getty Images: 28 left;
Hulton Archive/Getty Images: 7, 9, 14, 15, 17, 21, 24 left, 24 right, 31, 32, 36; Library of Congress: 13, 19, 35;
North Wind Picture Archives: 6, 10, 20, 23, 34; Stock Montage: 27 left, 27 right, 30.

Library of Congress Cataloging-in-Publication Data

De Capua, Sarah.
Abolitionists : a force for change / by Sarah E. De Capua.
p. cm. — (Journey to freedom)
Summary: Briefly describes the accomplishments of American abolitionists from
the seventeenth through the nineteenth centuries as they struggled to end slavery.
ISBN 1-56766-644-2 (Library Bound : alk. paper)
1. Abolitionists—United States—History—Juvenile literature. 2. Antislavery movements—United States—
History—Juvenile literature. 3. Slavery—United States—History—Juvenile literature. 4. African Americans—
History—To 1853—Juvenile literature. [1. Abolitionists. 2. Antislavery movements. 3. Slavery.
4. African Americans—History—To 1853.] I. Title. II. Series.
E449 .D28 2002
326'.8'0973—dc21

2002002862

Contents

THE U.S. HOUSE OF REPRESENTATIVES PASSING THE THIRTEENTH
AMENDMENT. THIS AMENDMENT WAS RATIFIED BY CONGRESS ON DECEMBER
6, 1865, AND OFFICIALLY PUT AN END TO SLAVERY IN THE UNITED STATES.

Slavery in the United States

"Neither slavery nor **involuntary servitude** . . . shall exist within the United States. . . ."

These words are from the Thirteenth Amendment to the United States Constitution. The amendment was ratified, or officially agreed upon, by the U.S. **Congress** on December 6, 1865. The amendment ended slavery in the United States forever.

These words, however, were not just an addition to the Constitution, the document that gives us the principles by which the United States is governed. They marked the end of a long struggle for freedom waged by black Americans and white Americans on behalf of black slaves. The struggle lasted more than 200 years and was one of the reasons for the American Civil War (1861–1865).

THE BATTLE OF GETTYSBURG DURING THE U.S. CIVIL WAR. THE ISSUE OF SLAVERY WAS ONE REASON THE NORTH AND THE SOUTH FACED EACH OTHER IN BATTLE.

The first blacks who arrived in what was to become the United States did so in the 1600s as **indentured servants.** They pledged to work for the person or family who paid their way across the ocean for a period of about seven years. When the agreed-upon number of years was completed, most blacks took their places in their communities. They became respected, contributing members of society.

By the end of the 1600s, indentured servitude was no longer a choice, however. Black people from Africa and the Caribbean were kidnapped, chained, and brought to the **colonies** as unwilling servants and laborers for white settlers in the North and the South.

In the early 1800s, slavery virtually ended in the northern United States. As the region's **economy** grew to depend on manufacturing, slave labor on farms became less necessary. The number of northern blacks, free or enslaved, was less than 60,000—a fraction of the white population. And laws were being written in nearly every northern state to abolish slavery altogether.

SLAVES BEING TRANSPORTED SOUTH AFTER BEING PURCHASED IN RICHMOND, VIRGINIA. AT AUCTIONS, SLAVES WERE BOUGHT AND SOLD LIKE LIVESTOCK.

The agricultural economy in the South, though, was almost totally dependent on slave labor. By 1860, when the total U.S. population was 31 million, almost 4 million slaves lived in the South. Southern landowners insisted that slavery was a cherished way of life. They argued that if slavery were abolished, or permanently ended, the South's economy would be ruined.

As Americans in the North and the South struggled over the legal right to own slaves, groups called abolitionists focused on the **moral** right to own slaves. Since before the country's beginnings, when it was just a loosely knit collection of colonies, abolitionists had insisted that it was **immoral** for one human being to own another. Their goal was to end slavery in the United States forever.

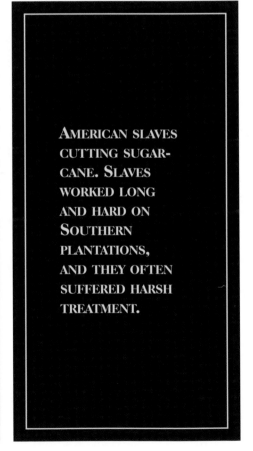

AMERICAN SLAVES CUTTING SUGAR-CANE. SLAVES WORKED LONG AND HARD ON SOUTHERN PLANTATIONS, AND THEY OFTEN SUFFERED HARSH TREATMENT.

The first people to speak out forcefully in favor of abolition were members of the Religious Order of the Society of Friends, also known as Quakers. The religion's founder, George Fox, began speaking of abolition in the mid-1600s. The Quakers stressed that slavery was a violation of God's law for mankind. In the years that saw the struggle for freedom for all Americans, abolitionists found a variety of ways to spread their message. These methods included individuals who spoke to audiences of supporters; newspapers and organizations that advanced the cause; and the Underground Railroad, which helped slaves escape.

GEORGE FOX, THE FOUNDER OF THE RELIGIOUS ORDER OF THE SOCIETY OF FRIENDS. KNOWN ALSO AS QUAKERS, THIS GROUP WORKED TO END SLAVERY IN THE UNITED STATES.

Inspiring Individuals

Many people—blacks and whites, men and women—spoke out **eloquently** against slavery. Perhaps the best remembered are those who dedicated their lives to the abolitionist cause during the late 1700s and 1800s.

Some of the best-known abolitionists were themselves former slaves. Richard Allen, Sojourner Truth, Frederick Douglass, and Harriet Tubman spoke of their experiences as slaves to help audiences understand the injustices that they, and other slaves, faced.

Richard Allen (1760–1831) was born into slavery in Philadelphia. In 1780, he paid his owner $2,000 for his own freedom. He spent his years as a freeman working and preaching. He became a Methodist minister in 1782, and began preaching at Philadelphia's St. George's Methodist Church in 1786. Soon after, Allen founded the Free African Society. The society worked to provide spiritual guidance, education, and health care to blacks.

In 1816, Allen helped establish the African Methodist Episcopal (AME) Church. Allen believed that black members of society should have their own church in which to worship. Today, African Methodist Episcopal churches can be found throughout the United States.

RICHARD ALLEN (CENTER) WAS BORN INTO SLAVERY. AFTER BUYING HIS FREEDOM, HE FOUNDED THE FREE AFRICAN SOCIETY AND HELPED ESTABLISH THE AFRICAN METHODIST EPISCOPAL CHURCH.

Sojourner Truth (1797?–1883) was freed from slavery when the state of New York passed an **emancipation** law that became effective on July 4, 1827. Deeply religious, Truth was at first a preacher. By 1851, she was a popular speaker at abolitionist **conventions** in New England. Another abolitionist, William Lloyd Garrison, had convinced her to join him on a lecture tour. As a slave, she did not learn to read or write, so she dictated her **autobiography,** called *Narrative of Sojourner Truth,* to a friend in 1850. She believed in using nonviolent methods to end slavery.

SOJOURNER TRUTH WAS FREED FROM SLAVERY IN 1827. FIRST A PREACHER, SHE BECAME A WELL-KNOWN ABOLITIONIST SPEAKER AND OFTEN GAVE LECTURES WITH WILLIAM LLOYD GARRISON.

Frederick Douglass (1818–1895) was an escaped slave who became the most famous black man of his day, as well as one of the most popular speakers in the abolitionist movement. He published three autobiographies, *Narrative of the Life of Frederick Douglass, My Bondage and My Freedom,* and *The Life and Times of Frederick Douglass.* Douglass also published his own antislavery newspaper, the *North Star.*

FREDERICK DOUGLASS ESCAPED FROM SLAVERY AND BECAME A POPULAR SPEAKER IN THE ABOLITIONIST MOVEMENT. HIS NEWSPAPER, THE *NORTH STAR,* PROVIDED NEWS AND INSPIRATION FOR THOSE IN THE ANTISLAVERY CAUSE.

arriet Tubman (1820–1913) is known as the Moses of her people. Like the biblical Moses who led the Israelites out of slavery in Egypt, Tubman led blacks out of slavery in the South. She escaped from slavery in 1849 and spent the following ten years guiding more than 300 slaves to freedom on the **Underground Railroad.** After the Civil War (1861–1865), she spent the rest of her life speaking out about these experiences and supporting other important issues, such as women's rights.

HARRIET TUBMAN IN **1860.** KNOWN AS THE MOSES OF HER PEOPLE, TUBMAN ESCAPED FROM SLAVERY IN **1849** AND THEN HELPED MORE THAN **300** SLAVES FIND THEIR WAY TO FREEDOM.

Many abolitionists were neither black nor former slaves. A well-known white abolitionist, William Lloyd Garrison (1805–1879), was born in Massachusetts. He was indentured at age fourteen to a newspaper printer. As a result, he became an expert printer. Throughout Garrison's childhood, he was troubled by the enslavement of blacks. As he grew older, he wrote countless articles calling slavery immoral. These articles helped to influence people in the North to abolish slavery.

WILLIAM LLOYD GARRISON, A WELL-KNOWN SPEAKER AND PRINTER, DURING THE ABOLITION MOVEMENT. HE BELIEVED IN COMPLETE AND IMMEDIATE FREEDOM FOR SLAVES.

Some abolitionists believed in freeing the slaves gradually over time. Garrison believed in complete and immediate freedom for all slaves. He became a prominent spokesman for the abolitionist cause and was a featured speaker at conventions throughout the North. Garrison also established newspapers and organizations to help further abolition.

Some abolitionists did not believe in ending slavery by peaceful methods, or by escaping when possible. They believed in using force when necessary, and they encouraged slaves to rebel against their owners. Nat Turner and John Brown led famous slave revolts. Though unsuccessful, the revolts shed light on the urgent need many Americans felt to free the slaves.

WILLIAM LLOYD GARRISON BEING ATTACKED AT AN ABOLITIONIST MEETING. GARRISON'S VIEWS ENCOURAGED SOME PEOPLE WHILE ANGERING THOSE WHO DISAGREED WITH HIM.

Nat Turner (1800–1831) became the most feared slave in America after he led a failed slave rebellion in Virginia. The uprising began at midnight on August 22, 1831, when Turner and four of his followers murdered six people on his owner's farm. The murdered people included Joseph Travis, Turner's owner, and Travis's wife. Turner and his followers then stole horses and rode from farm to farm, where they were joined by more slaves. By the following day, sixty slaves had joined the rebellion. By the time law-enforcement authorities crushed the rebellion late in the day on August 23, at least fifty-seven white people, including women and infants, had been murdered.

A SCENE FROM NAT TURNER'S SLAVE REBELLION. OVER THE COURSE OF SIX DAYS, TURNER AND SIXTY SLAVES MURDERED AT LEAST FIFTY-SEVEN PEOPLE.

For more than two months, Turner hid in the woods to avoid capture. He was finally caught on October 30, 1831. He stood trial for the **insurrection** on November 5. When the trial was over, Turner was found guilty and sentenced to death. He was hanged on November 11, 1831. Twenty other rebels were hanged as well. The result of Turner's failed rebellion was harsher treatment of slaves by owners, who feared that their slaves, too, would rise up against them. In spite of this harsher treatment, many slaves and free blacks saw Nat Turner as a hero. Later abolitionists considered him to be a **martyr** to their cause.

NAT TURNER WAS FINALLY CAUGHT AFTER HIDING IN THE WOODS FOR TWO MONTHS. HE STOOD TRIAL, WAS FOUND GUILTY, AND WAS SENTENCED TO DEATH.

John Brown (1800–1859), a white man, was born and raised in Connecticut. In 1849, Brown and his family settled in the black community of North Elba, New York. Brown hated slavery and believed God was telling him to free every slave. In 1859, Brown devised a plan to capture the federal **arsenal** at Harpers Ferry, Virginia. He would give the guns stored there to slaves so they could fight for their freedom. Brown told his friend, Frederick Douglass, about the plan. Douglass tried unsuccessfully to convince Brown that the plan would not work.

JOHN BROWN LED A RAID ON HARPERS FERRY IN OCTOBER 1859. HIS HOPE WAS TO SEIZE THE GUNS AT THE ARSENAL AND GIVE THEM TO SLAVES SO THEY COULD FIGHT FOR THEIR FREEDOM.

Brown's raid on Harpers Ferry began on October 16, 1859, when he led a band of eighteen men to seize the arsenal. They succeeded, but a two-day standoff with U.S. Marines led to the death of two of Brown's sons. Brown was captured, tried, and convicted of **treason,** insurrection, and murder. (A railroad guard on a bridge to Harpers Ferry was killed by one of Brown's men, and a wounded marine later died.) Brown was sentenced to death and hanged on December 2, 1859. Harriet Tubman mourned his loss, calling him the "Savior of our People."

Henry Highland Garnet (1815–1882) was born a slave in Maryland. When he was nine years old, his owner died and Garnet's father began planning the family's escape to freedom in the North. The family traveled along the Underground Railroad until they reached New York City. In 1842, Garnet became a minister. He used his sermons to preach about the evils of slavery and shared his ideas about what his fellow blacks could do to help end it. He also wrote newspaper articles that reflected his opinions.

Garnet believed slavery would not end without violence and political action. He urged slaves to kill their owners. He delivered a famous speech at the 1843 National Negro Convention in Buffalo, New York. In it, he urged slaves everywhere to resist their **oppressors.** Garnet insisted that it was better to "die freemen than live to be slaves." After the passage of the Thirteenth Amendment, Garnet's work to support abolition shifted to getting equality for blacks.

OPPOSITE: JOHN BROWN ON HIS WAY TO HIS EXECUTION ON DECEMBER 2, 1859. AFTER THE RAID, HE WAS CAPTURED AND CONVICTED OF TREASON, MURDER, AND INSURRECTION.

Other individuals who devoted themselves to the cause of ending slavery in the United States included Mary Ann Shadd Cary, Wendell Phillips, Maria Stewart, and William Still.

WENDELL PHILLIPS (LEFT) WAS A WELL-KNOWN SPEAKER FOR THE ABOLITIONIST MOVEMENT. WILLIAM STILL (RIGHT) KEPT NOTES ABOUT HIS WORK ON THE UNDERGROUND RAILROAD THAT WERE PUBLISHED AS *STILL'S UNDERGROUND RAIL ROAD NOTES* IN 1871.

The Underground Railroad

Legend tells of a runaway slave named Tice Davids, who escaped from his owner's Kentucky farm in 1831. With his owner pursuing him in order to recapture him, Davids swam across the Ohio River. He emerged from the river in the town of Ripley. Ripley was located in Ohio, a Free State. A white man who lived in the town hid Davids in his basement.

Davids's owner searched the town for hours. He finally gave up, saying, "Davids must have gone off on some underground railroad." This is the first time the term "underground railroad" was used. It was not a real railroad, but the people involved in it used railroad terms. Houses where the slaves were hidden were called "stations." The owners of the houses were called "stationmasters." Guides were called "conductors." The runaway slaves were called "passengers."

ONE OF THE MANY HOMES USED ON THE UNDERGROUND RAILROAD. THESE HOUSES, WHICH WERE USED TO HIDE SLAVES, WERE CALLED "STATIONS."

It was against the law to help runaway slaves, so there was no single leader of the movement. Stations were kept secret. Most members of the Underground Railroad did not know each other, but their goal was to abolish slavery in the United States. While many worked by day to achieve that goal, all worked by night to take fugitive slaves into their homes. They hid the slaves in their basements, their attics, or in the secret passageways of their homes. Other hiding places included rooms with removable floorboards, wagons with false bottoms, and barns with hidden basements. Slaves could rest in these hiding places. Stationmasters gave the escaped slaves food and other supplies. When it was time for the fugitives to move on to the next station, they traveled north to the Free States and to Canada.

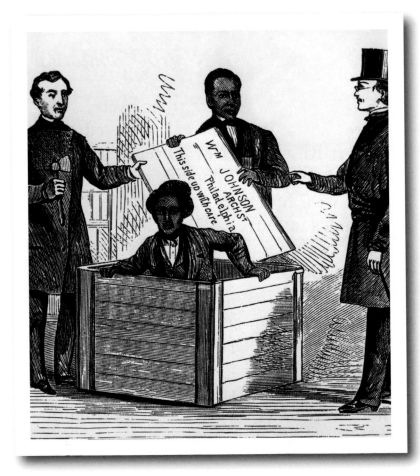

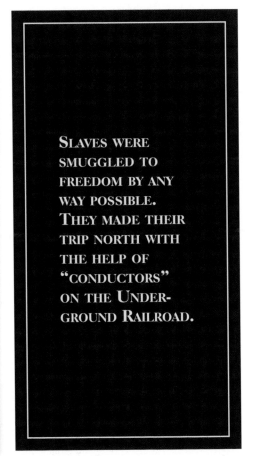

SLAVES WERE SMUGGLED TO FREEDOM BY ANY WAY POSSIBLE. THEY MADE THEIR TRIP NORTH WITH THE HELP OF "CONDUCTORS" ON THE UNDERGROUND RAILROAD.

Blacks and whites worked together to help slaves on the Underground Railroad. The Indiana home of Levi Coffin and his wife, Catherine, is today one of the best-known stations on the Underground Railroad. Over many years, hundreds of runaway slaves found safety in the Coffin house.

Thomas Garrett's home in Delaware also was an Underground Railroad station. During the years it served as a station, about 2,500 slaves were hidden there. One of the slaves was Harriet Tubman. Tubman went on to be a conductor on the Underground Railroad and guided more than 300 slaves to freedom.

LEVI (LEFT) AND CATHERINE (RIGHT) COFFIN OFFERED THEIR HOME AS A STATION ON THE UNDERGROUND RAILROAD. THEY HELPED HUNDREDS OF SLAVES FIND SAFETY IN THE NORTH.

Lyman Beecher's home in Cincinnati, Ohio, was also a station. His daughter, Harriet Beecher Stowe, helped him. In 1852, Stowe published *Uncle Tom's Cabin*, the story of a black slave woman who escapes from her owner with her baby. Readers of the book learned of the cruelty and injustice of slavery. The novel gave strength to the abolitionist movement and is still considered to be one of the causes of the Civil War.

THE OHIO HOME OF LYMAN BEECHER (LEFT) WAS A STATION ON THE UNDERGROUND RAILROAD. HIS DAUGHTER, HARRIET BEECHER STOWE (RIGHT), HELPED AT THE STATION AND WROTE *UNCLE TOM'S CABIN*, A FAMOUS BOOK ABOUT SLAVERY.

Frederick Douglass operated a station from his newspaper office in Rochester, New York. Many slaves traveled through Douglass's station.

Jermain Loguen was another runaway slave who served as a stationmaster. He hid about 1,500 escaped slaves in his New York home.

William Still was a free black man who lived in Philadelphia, Pennsylvania. Still worked on the Underground Railroad and, in spite of the danger of being caught, kept notes about his experiences. His notes were published in 1871 as a book called *Still's Underground Rail Road Notes.* It is one of the most famous books ever published about the Underground Railroad.

Today, many houses on the Underground Railroad have been preserved and are now open as museums. Each year, thousands of visitors tour these former stations. Houses in states such as Ohio, Pennsylvania, Indiana, and Delaware are among those that continue to serve as reminders of the abolitionist movement.

Newspapers Champion the Cause

Without radio or television, newspapers were the most significant means of keeping current with the important issues and events of life in the United States. The issue of slavery appeared often, especially in newspapers located in northern and southern cities.

Newspapers devoted to bringing the abolitionist cause to as many readers as possible sprang up throughout the North. They were read widely by both blacks and whites.

In 1821, Benjamin Lundy began publishing the antislavery newspaper, the *Genius of Universal Emancipation.* Lundy, a Quaker living in Baltimore, Maryland, published the newspaper from 1821 to 1835. Lundy moved to Illinois in 1839 and once again began publishing the *Genius of Universal Emancipation.* He continued to publish it until his death later that same year.

THE

GENIUS OF UNIVERSAL EMANCIPATION

AND

Quarterly Anti-Slavery Review.

BY BENJAMIN LUNDY.

FIAT JUSTITIA   RUAT CŒLUM.

NUMBER I. VOL. I.—FIFTH SERIES.

JULY, 1837.

THE *GENIUS OF UNIVERSAL EMANCIPATION* WAS AN ANTISLAVERY NEWSPAPER PUBLISHED BY BENJAMIN LUNDY.

William Lloyd Garrison published newspapers with the purpose of convincing slaveholders that they were evil and that slavery was sinful. Garrison's best-known newspaper was the *Liberator,* which was published from 1831 to 1865. Frederick Douglass considered this newspaper second only to the Bible in its importance to his life.

A newspaper called the *Colored American* was established in 1837 and was edited by Samuel D. Cornish. The articles of Henry Highland Garnet, a free black committed to ending slavery, were often featured in the paper. The *Colored American* focused on abolitionist and slavery issues until 1841, its last year of publication.

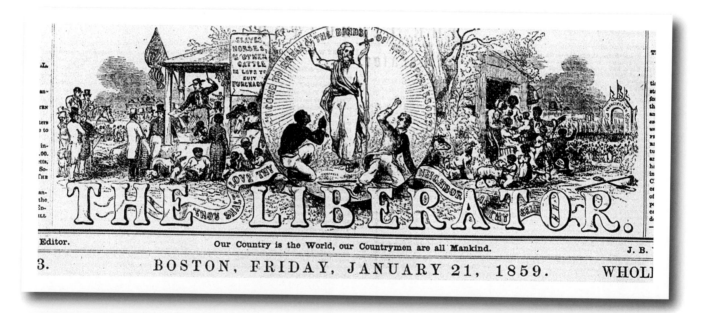

THE *LIBERATOR* WAS WILLIAM LLOYD GARRISON'S BEST-KNOWN NEWSPAPER. IT WAS PUBLISHED FROM 1831 TO 1865.

The *National Anti-Slavery Standard* was a weekly newspaper published by Lydia Maria Child and her husband David. It was published in New York from 1841 to 1870.

The *North Star* was published in Rochester, New York, from 1847 to 1851 by Frederick Douglass. The first issue appeared on December 3, 1847. Douglass edited and published newspapers for the next twenty-five years. The *North Star* allowed him to further express his abolitionist views.

The *Anti-Slavery Reporter* was published in New York City during the 1840s by the American and Foreign Anti-Slavery Society. The paper would accept cash contributions toward its expenses only from people who did not earn their money through slavery.

Among the many other antislavery newspapers were the *Free Enquirer, Pennsylvania Freeman,* and *Freedom's Journal,* the first newspaper in the United States published entirely by blacks. All of these papers sought to reach as many readers as possible with the plight of the enslaved.

The need for abolitionist newspapers ended with the passage of the Thirteenth Amendment. During the existence of these and other, smaller papers, however, they were an important voice for abolition.

LYDIA MARIA CHILD, PUBLISHER OF THE *NATIONAL ANTI-SLAVERY STANDARD.* SHE AND HER HUSBAND DAVID PRODUCED THE PAPER FROM 1841 TO 1870.

Abolitionists Organize

Since the beginning of slavery in America, people spoke out against it. As more and more people saw the injustice of slavery, they formed groups, or organizations, to make their views known publicly and to help bring attention to the abolitionist cause. Many small societies and organizations existed throughout the 1700s. In 1786, Benjamin Franklin became the first president of the Pennsylvania Society for Promoting the Abolition of Slavery. The best-known organizations, however, came into existence in the fifty years before the Civil War.

BENJAMIN FRANKLIN WAS ONE OF THE NATION'S FIRST ABOLITIONISTS. IN 1786, HE BECAME PRESIDENT OF THE PENNSYLVANIA SOCIETY FOR PROMOTING THE ABOLITION OF SLAVERY .

In 1816, the American Colonization Society was founded. Formed in Washington, D.C., the society sought to provide money for the **emigration** of black people to Africa. Members and supporters of the organization believed that blacks brought to the United States, or their **descendants,** should be returned to Africa. The West African nation of Liberia was established by the American Colonization Society in 1822 as a permanent home for freed U.S. slaves.

The American Society of Free Persons of Color was founded in Philadelphia, Pennsylvania, in 1830. It was formed to oppose the work of the American Colonization Society. The society's members focused on abolishing slavery and making life better for freed blacks in the United States. It also made plans to establish a community in Canada for blacks who wanted to escape discrimination in the United States.

SOME ABOLITIONISTS FAVORED RETURNING SLAVES TO AFRICA. THIS SHIP, THE DANISH STEAMER *HORSA*, TOOK 200 U.S. SLAVES TO LIBERIA, A NATION IN WEST AFRICA.

William Lloyd Garrison, the publisher of the *Liberator,* founded the American Anti-Slavery Society in Massachusetts in 1833. Garrison and his followers in the organization (often called Garrisonians) believed in abolishing slavery through persuasion, convincing slave owners that their practices were morally wrong. The American Anti-Slavery Society encouraged lectures and the publication of newspapers and other printed materials to achieve that goal. Members did not believe that political measures would bring about the end of slavery.

The American and Foreign Anti-Slavery Society was formed in 1840. Founded by Arthur and Lewis Tappan in Rochester, New York, it was made up of former members of Garrison's American Anti-Slavery Society.

In 1858, the African Civilization Society was founded by Henry Highland Garnet, the founder of the *Colored American* newspaper, and another black leader, Martin Delany. Based in New York City, the society hoped to end slavery by encouraging blacks to resettle in Africa, where they could grow cotton. Members of the African Civilization Society argued that the competition with the South's most important and profitable crop, which was also cotton, would eventually end the need for slavery in the South.

THE ABOLITIONIST MOVEMENT HAD MANY NOTABLE LEADERS, BUT FEW WERE MORE FAMOUS THAN FREDERICK DOUGLASS (CENTER).

Major cities in the North also established their own anti-slavery societies. Such cities included Philadelphia, New York, and Boston.

By the end of the 1850s, in spite of the efforts of abolitionist individuals, groups, and publications—or perhaps because of them—it became clear that the United States was heading for an actual battle against slavery. It took the Civil War, the **Emancipation Proclamation** of 1863, and the Thirteenth Amendment to accomplish what many abolitionists had spent their lives trying to achieve.

PRESIDENT ABRAHAM LINCOLN (THIRD FROM LEFT), SIGNING THE EMANCIPATION PROCLAMATION ON JANUARY 1, 1863. THIS LAW FREED THE SLAVES IN THE REBELLING STATES DURING THE CIVIL WAR.

Timeline

1600s	The first blacks arrive as indentured servants in what is now the United States.
1700	Slavery is an established institution in the North and the South.
1760	Richard Allen is born a slave in Philadelphia.
1786	Benjamin Franklin becomes the first president of the Pennsylvania Society for Promoting the Abolition of Slavery.
1797?	Sojourner Truth is born into slavery in New York.
1800s	Slavery ends in the North.
1800	Nat Turner is born a slave in Virginia. John Brown is born in Connecticut.
1805	William Lloyd Garrison is born in Massachusetts.
1815	Henry Highland Garnet is born into slavery in Maryland.
1816	Richard Allen helps to establish the African Methodist Episcopal (AME) Church. The American Colonization Society is founded.
1818	Frederick Douglass is born into slavery in Maryland.
1820	Harriet Tubman is born a slave in Maryland.
1821	Benjamin Lundy begins publishing *Genius of Universal Emancipation*.
1827	New York abolishes slavery.
1830	The American Society of Free Persons of Color is founded.
1831	Nat Turner leads an unsuccessful slave rebellion in Virginia on August 22. Garrison begins publishing the *Liberator*.
1833	Garrison founds the American Anti-Slavery Society.
1837	The *Colored American* newspaper is established.
1840s	The *Anti-Slavery Reporter* is published in New York City.
1840	Arthur and Lewis Tappan establish the American and Foreign Anti-Slavery Society.
1841	The *National Anti-Slavery Standard* is published in New York.
1843	Henry Highland Garnet speaks at the National Negro Convention in Buffalo, New York.
1847	Frederick Douglass begins publishing the *North Star*.
1858	The African Civilization Society is established.
1859	John Brown's raid on Harpers Ferry, Virginia, begins on October 16.
1861	The Civil War begins.
1863	President Abraham Lincoln issues the Emancipation Proclamation on January 1.
1865	The Civil War ends. The Thirteenth Amendment to the Constitution is ratified.

Glossary

arsenal (AHR-suh-nuhl)
An arsenal is a storage place for weapons and ammunition.

autobiography (aw-toh-by-OG-ruh-fee)
An autobiography is a book in which the author tells the story of his or her life.

colonies (KOL-uh-neez)
Colonies are territories controlled by another country.

Congress (KONG-griss)
Congress is the U.S. government body that makes laws. It is made up of the House of Representatives and the Senate.

conventions (kuhn-VEN-shuhns)
Conventions are large gatherings of people who have the same interests.

descendants (di-SEND-uhnts)
Descendants are someone's children, grandchildren, and so on.

economy (ee-KON-uh-mee)
An economy is the way a country or state runs its industry, trade, or finance.

eloquently (EL-uh-kwuhnt-lee)
Someone who speaks eloquently has a smooth, clear voice.

emancipation (i-man-si-PAY-shuhn)
Emancipation is the act of freeing a person or group from slavery or control.

**Emancipation Proclamation
(i-man-si-PAY-shuhn prok-luh-MAY-shuhn)**
The Emancipation Proclamation is the law signed by President Abraham Lincoln on January 1, 1863, that freed the slaves in the rebelling states.

emigration (em-uh-GRAY-shuhn)
Emigration is the act of leaving one country in order to live permanently in another.

immoral (i-MOR-uhl)
An immoral person has no sense of right and wrong.

**indentured servants
(in-DEN-churd SUR-vuhnts)**
Indentured servants are person who sign a contract to work for a certain period of time in return for payment of travel expenses.

insurrection (in-suh-REK-shuhn)
An insurrection is a revolt against a government.

**involuntary servitude
(in-VOL-uhn-ter-ee SEHR-vuh-tyood)**
A person in involuntary servitude is denied the freedom to make his or her own choices.

martyr (MAR-tur)
A martyr is someone who is killed or made to suffer because of his or her beliefs.

moral (MOR-uhl)
A moral person is be able to distinguish right from wrong.

oppressors (uh-PRESS-uhrs)
Oppressors are people who are cruel to others.

treason (TREE-zuhn)
Treason is the crime of betraying one's country.

**Underground Railroad
(UHN-dur-ground RAYL-rohd)**
The Underground Railroad was a collection of safe hiding places, usually the homes of abolitionists, for blacks escaping from the South to new homes in the Free Northern States or in Canada.

Index

For Further Reading

Books

Feelings, Tom. *The Middle Passage: White Ships Black Cargo.* New York: Dial Books for Young Readers, 1995.

January, Brendan. *The Emancipation Proclamation.* Danbury, Conn.: Children's Press, 1997.

Lasky, Kathryn. *True North: A Novel of the Underground Railroad.* New York: Scholastic, 1996.

Taylor, Kimberly Hayes. *Black Abolitionists and Freedom Fighters.* Minneapolis: The Oliver Press, 1996.

Thomas, Velma Maia. *Lest We Forget: The Passage from Africa to Slavery and Emancipation.* New York: Crown Publishers, 1997.

Web Sites

Visit our homepage for lots of links about abolitionists: *http://www.childsworld.com/links.html*

Note to Parents, Teachers, and Librarians:
We routinely verify our Web links to make sure they're safe, active sites—so encourage your readers to check them out!

About the Author

Born and raised in Connecticut, Sarah De Capua has always been fascinated by the work of those on the Underground Railroad. While researching this book, she had the opportunity to visit several houses that served as stations on the railroad. Ms. De Capua has written more than a dozen books for young readers. She resides in Colorado.